E. Jeffrey's

Lake District Sketchbook

45p.

E. Jeffrey's
Lake District Sketchbook

DALESMAN BOOKS
1972

The Dalesman Publishing Company Ltd.,
Clapham (via Lancaster), Yorkshire
First Published 1972

ISBN: 0 85206 162 5

Printed in Great Britain by Galava Printing Co. Ltd.,
Hallam Road, Nelson, Lancs.

Contents

The cover picture is of the Langdale Pikes from near Blea Tarn. Many of the sketches are based on photographs taken by W. R. Mitchell.

Introduction

THIS BOOK is more than a collection of black and white drawings of Lakeland. It is a vivid view in depth of a unique corner of Britain, its physical background through the year, its people at home and at work, its peaceful places and its wild life through the eyes of an artist who has had a unique experience as a painter and illustrator.

After an art training interrupted by army service during the first world war and a false start as a book-keeper in industry, Edward Jeffrey launched himself into commercial art in the Newcastle studio of a process engraver, where he learned not only the technique of advertising and catalogue and book jacket design but the highly skilled methods by which these are converted into printed form. Ten years of this qualified him to move to similar work at a London commercial studio until the second world war closed the firm. Following a spell of A.R.P. activity he came north again to Yorkshire to undertake publicity work for an engineering firm and also the designing of book jackets for many well-known publishers.

Then came an unusual interlude. He was invited by a London publisher to create a children's character for a series of colour books, and Toby Twire was born—an active little pig dressed in red rompers with a patch on the knee, based on a soft toy his wife was making at the time. More work on juvenile books followed and he moved to his present home at Ravenstonedale where designs for annuals, painting books and pop-up novelties poured from his fertile mind. When the post-war period brought the take-over of publishers and a change of fashion in children's books, Edward Jeffrey moved into yet another field of art work, the design and painting of inn signs (they can be found all over the north country), and the designing of greetings cards for Messrs Valentines of Dundee, where his beautiful bird and landscape studies took him into the "top ten" for sales.

Yet through all this varied professional career he continued to pursue his first love of landscape drawing and water colour painting. His work has appeared at the exhibitions of the Royal British Artists, the Royal Welsh Academy and the Royal Scottish Academy, as well as at provincial shows at Newcastle, Huddersfield, Stockton-on-Tees, Grasmere and Kendal. He is a member of the Lake Artists

Society and the Kendal Art Society, and his water colour paintings are to be found in private collections all over the world. His delightful colour covers for the magazine *Cumbria* are widely appreciated, as are his drawings of the Lakeland scene, its people and their varied activities, which are the subject of this attractive sketch book.

From his charming old world studio (converted stable buildings) at Ravenstonedale, where as he works he can watch the birds in the trees and at his bird table outside, and from his journeys into the towns, villages and quiet places of Lakeland, his perceptive pen shares his enthusiasm, his knowledge and his skill with a great company who enjoy the riches of the scene, the landmarks, and the heritage of this delightful area.

HARRY J. SCOTT

1.   Three Lakes

MORE THAN A dozen major lakes radiate from the core of the Cumbrian Mountains in blue-spoke formation. Three of these—Windermere, Ullswater and Derwentwater—command perhaps the greatest attention by virtue of their size and situation.

Windermere, although less than a mile in breadth at its widest point, is over ten miles long. It is also the most easily accessible of the lakes to visitors from the south. One of its most popular attractions is the service of diesel-powered "steamers" operated between Waterhead (Ambleside) and Lakeside (Newby Bridge). The sketches opposite show the *Teal* (once rather uncharitably described as "a perambulating wedding cake"), members of its crew, and the landing stages at Lakeside and Bowness.

Much more hum-drum is the ferry service which the good ship *Drake* (page 10) operates across a 700 yard reach of Windermere near Bowness. Although the "voyage" only takes five minutes, there has been at least one occasion when a passenger has attempted to book a berth!

TEAL
BARROW

BOWNESS PIER

Windermere
64

9

Windermere Ferry

PASSENGERS ENTERING ON OR LEAVING THE BOAT WHILST IN MOTION DO SO AT THEIR OWN RISK

LAST BOAT LEAVES 8.50 FERRY HOUSE SIDE AT
LAST FERRY LEAVES NAB SIDE AT 9.0 P.M. SATURDAYS ONLY

THE OTHER LAKE with a regular "steamer "service is Ullswater —seven miles long with a distinct dog's leg curve in the centre. The *Raven* (page 13) plies between Glenridding and Pooley Bridge, offering passengers some splendid views of the surrounding mountains. One of these mountains, the 2154 ft. Place Fell, forms the centrepiece of the scraperboard study on page 12. In the sketch below are some of the wild deer which still range over the Martindale fells to the east of Ullswater.

Derwentwater, "the Queen of the English Lakes," is depicted in the centre sketch on page 14. This study also shows greylag geese, which after a long absence have now returned to Lakeland as nesting birds. In the lower sketch they are seen in close-up on Millom Marsh.

2.   On View

THE LAKE DISTRICT, by virtue of its mountainous terrain, is not rich in stately homes. Most of these architectural extravaganzas are to be found on the fringes of the area, two of the best known being at Levens and Holker on the southern perimeter of Lakeland.

Levens Hall (below and page 16) has as one of its major attractions what is claimed to be "the only collection of stationary engines in Britain regularly running under steam." It also boasts two full-size traction engines—*Bertha*, a Fowler showman's engine, is shown in the sketch on page 16. The figure to the right is Mr. Robin Bagot, owner of the hall, and behind him is some of the topiary for which Levens is famous.

Holker Hall (page 17) is noted for the rhododendrons of its gardens and the deer of its park as well as for the contents of the house. It is visited by more than 50,000 people a year.

LEVENS HALL GARDENS KENDAL

Holker Hall

VIRTUALLY ALL the homes on view in central Lakeland are relatively small and have literary associations. One of the most fascinating is Hill Top at Near Sawrey (below and opposite), the home of Beatrix Potter from 1904 to 1943. It remains very much as it was in her time, and somehow is still peopled by the characters she created—Mrs. Tiggy-Winkle, Jeminah Puddleduck and the three bad mice.

A rather different building which is on view to the public is the Courthouse near Hawkshead (page 20). Built by Furness Abbey, it has survived down the centuries virtually unaltered. Now owned by the National Trust, it is leased to the Museum of Lakeland Life and Industry and contains a remarkable collection of Hawkshead bygones.

19

3.   Towns and Villages

THE LAKE COUNTIES contain only two really large settlements
—Barrow and Carlisle. But what its towns lack in size they make up
for in age and character.

   Typifying them is Appleby (below), the ancient county town of
Westmorland, with its superb main street leading up from the
church past the crosses and moot hall to the castle at the top. The
sketches on page 22 are of the town's hospital of St. Anne, founded
by Lady Anne Clifford in 1652.

FOUNTAINS
YARD

SATAN
IN
BONDS

THE
BUTTER
MARKET

OLD
GRAMMAR
SCHOOL AND
PARISH CHURCH

KIRKBY STEPHEN

Above: Some of the main historical features of Kirkby Stephen. "Satan in Bonds" is a fragment of a Saxon cross in the church, which boasts some magnificent 13th century arcades.

Kendal (above), the administrative centre of Westmorland, is noted
for the remains of its castle (top, right). Here was born Katherine
Parr, Henry VIII's sixth wife. Also shown in this sketch are the
town hall, Abbot Hall and the parish church.

Whitehaven (opposite) was at one time the largest settlement in the
North after York and Newcastle. It retains several relics of its former
importance, as well as boasting a flourishing harbour trade.

MDCCXXX

Whitehaven

25

IT IS IN the villages rather than the towns that the traveller makes his contact with the real Lakeland—its moods, its customs and its people.

Uldale (below) epitomises the type of village which has not been corrupted by tourism. It is sited "back o' Skidda,' " on the northern edge of the National Park four miles north-east of Bassenthwaite Lake.

Dacre and Lorton (opposite) are more central but nevertheless still relatively unspoilt. Dacre, near Ullswater, has a 14th century castle which has been restored as a private house. Lorton lies between Crummock Water and Cockermouth. Its "Horse Shoe Inn' will have welcomed generations of travellers doing the round journey over Honister and Whinlatter passes.

ULDALE

DACRE

Horse Shoe INN LORTON

Many famous men have been born in the Lake Counties. One of the most distinguished was Professor John Dalton who propounded the Atomic Theory. His birthplace at Eaglesfield, near Cockermouth, still retains its spiral stone staircase (right).

c . j e f f r e y

THE HIGH CHAPEL

RAVENSTONEDALE

St. OSWALD'S
CHURCH

BASE OF
SAXON
CROSS

TARN HOUSE
1664

c. jeffrey

Ravenstonedale, where Mr. Jeffrey has lived since 1947, lies between Tebay and Kirkby Stephen. It boasts many interesting buildings, including a church with a three-decker pulpit. Tarn House, a mile from the village, retains its medieval windows and Jacobean doorway.

28

PETTY HALL

GB 1604 MB

Orton

BELLS IN
THE NAVE OF
THE CHURCH

Orton, eight miles north-west of Ravenstonedale, is noted for its richly ornamented Elizabethan hall. The small church has a 15th century bell in its fine tower which was built well over 400 years ago.

4.   Lakeland Events

PERHAPS THE MOST notable thing about events in Lakeland is not so much their variety but the fact that so many are unique to the area. A large proportion of those illustrated on the following pages are not to be found elsewhere.

On pages 30–32 are sketches of Appleby Hill Fair, the great June gathering for gipsies and dealers from all over the country. Equally traditional but totally different in concept are Lakeland hunting events. Pages 33 and 34 respectively show meets of the Ullswater Pack and the Vale of Lune Harriers.

Once-a-year events naturally attract enormous interest. Eskdale Show (page 35), known as the "Herdwick Royal," is traditionally the time when Herdwick tups are hired out for the winter. Grasmere Sports (page 36), with its Cumbrian-style wrestling, can claim to be the main event in the Lakeland sporting calendar.

Hound trailing is peculiar to the north-west of England; the sketches on page 37 were made at a trial near Kendal. Also unusual in concept are the 17 mile walks across the shifting sands of Morecambe Bay from Hest Bank to Grange (page 38).

31

appleby

Ullswater 64

Eskdale 63

Kendal

37

Morecambe Bay

5.   People at Work

RURAL EMPLOYMENT in the Lake District is still heavily
dominated by farming. The sketch below and those on page 40
highlight one of the most fascinating events of the farming year—
sheep-shearing. These studies were made at Gatesgarth, a farm
between Buttermere and Honister, where the clipping of the 2,500
sheep is a month-long job.

More specialist and localised is the growing of damsons in the
Lyth Valley (page 41); thousands of trees thrive here because of the
underlying limestone and the sheltered position.

40

Lythe Valley

RECREATIONAL PURSUITS can also involve hard work. Few self-inflicted forms of exercise illustrate this more appropriately than the ascent of Scafell Pike (opposite)—at 3,210 feet England's highest mountain. These sketches show features encountered on the long climb from Seathwaite in Borrowdale to the rock-strewn summit. The drawing below shows a party of schoolboys fully equipped for mountaineering; they were climbing away from Ullswater towards the 2,800 feet Sticks Pass.

The horse has for centuries helped man to conserve energy—both in climbing up hills and moving over more level ground. A modern resurgance of this tradition is the cult of pony-trekking (page 44), which not surprisingly has the Lake District as one of its most popular centres.

The Lake District National Park warden has a full-time post but is actively involved with recreation (page 45). He has a Land Rover to give mobility in all conditions, and his many tasks range from way-marking to clearing undergrowth.

Scafell Pike
'65.

Herdwicks on way to Sty Head

FIRST AID STRETCHER

SEATHWAITE

Sty Head

The Summit

The Last Pull

Stockley Beck Bridge

43

44

6. Lakeland through the Year

LAKELAND, by virtue of its climatic extremes and extravagancies, has a wonderfully varied seasonal pattern. The twelve drawings on the succeeding pages show characteristic facets of the area month-by-month:

January: Robin; curling, winter aconites.

February: Ski-ing; rooks at the old nesting sites; snowdrops.

March: Walling; nest building; primrose.

April: Lambing; pussy willow; cowslips; Easter egg.

May: Swallow; horse chestnut; swill making; bluebells; mayfly.

June: Sailing; shearing; yellow flags.

July: Climbing; wild roses; harvest mice.

August: Art and handicraft exhibitions; blackcap on ash branch; wrestling at the sports.

September: Sports and shows; hazel nuts; red squirrel.

October: Brough Hill Fair; sycamore; stonechat.

November: Guy Fawkes; blue tits; stoat acquiring a white winter coat.

December: Village church; robin; Christmas roses.

JANUARY FEBRUARY

MARCH APRIL

49

JULY AUGUST

SEPTEMBER OCTOBER

NOVEMBER DECEMBER

7. Nature Reserves and Wild Life Parks

RECENT YEARS have seen a remarkable growth of interest in all aspects of wild life. Accompanying this has been a welcome move away from stuffed animals in dusty museum cases towards the exciting display of creatures in the semi-wild.

Typifying this trend in the Lake Counties has been the establishment of the Lowther Wildlife Park (page 54), only a few minutes drive from the M6. Here motorists can stretch their legs over 130 acres of lush grassland in the company of exotic birds and beasts.

The sketch below was made in Grizedale Forest and shows a basket in which wild duck are encouraged to lay their eggs. The Forestry Commission and eggs sound contradictory, but in fact Grizedale has pioneered ways in which the normal patterns of the countryside can exist hand-in-hand with timber production. Pages 55–7 depict aspects of the Forest, which contains a wildlife centre, a deer museum, forest walks and "tree tops" observation towers.

Grizedale Forest '64

55

Grisedale Forest

FALLOW DEER

SELECTION & CONTROL

DISTRIBUTION

GRIZEDALE FOREST

THE FOREST PROVIDES
A
PERPETUAL YIELD FOR ALL

FORESTRY
Timber production
and improvement
rural employment
broad leaved trees
conifers

FARMING
milk beef sheep
from sheltered and
fertile valley soils

← WILD LIFE CENTRE.

THE SCENERY of the Lake Counties is at its most spectacular in the centre, and hence here is to be found the greatest concentration of visitors. Conversely, the coastal regions are relatively uncrowded by man—and yet teeming with bird life. The coast is thus liberally sprinkled with nature reserves, including South Walney (opposite); Drigg Point, near Ravenglass (page 60); and Leighton Moss, near Silverdale (page 61). The sketch above is of a shelduck.

South Walney

Drigg Point 65

8.   Quiet Places

JUST AS WILDLIFE thrives away from the core of Lakeland, so do some of the communities and customs continue very much as they were fifty or more years ago. One hopes that the inclusion of such places in this book does not erode their precious qualities of peace and sincerity.

Roa Island (opposite) may seem a strange inclusion in a chapter on quiet places, for it is only five miles from Barrow. Yet, despite being tethered to the mainland by a causeway, it still retains much of its island nature. The sea seems to be all around, and the docks and industry to the north almost part of another world.

On page 64 are sketches of a gamekeeper and some of the many animals which come to feed at his hut in the woods to the west of Derwentwater. The study at the foot of this page is of a now vanished Lakeland industry—charcoal-burning in the coppice woods near Windermere. It will be familiar to all readers of "Swallows and Amazons."

EASTERN LAKELAND is one of the least known parts of the National Park, largely because it contains few through motoring routes. One of the many "cul-de-sac" valleys is Martindale, to the south of Ullswater, which retains the last deer-stalking forest in England (below, right; and page 66). Here is a herd of wild red deer whose ancestors would be seen by Romans using nearby High Street.

At the foot of the Martindale valley, almost on the eastern shore of Ullswater, is the tiny hamlet of Sandwick (below, left; and page 67). Buildings of the old Lakeland style of architecture fit comfortably in a setting of fell, woodland and lake.

The Greenside Valley (page 68) stretches west from Glenridding towards Helvellyn. Formerly noted for its lead mining, it is now a haven for fell walkers, skiers and youth hostellers.

MARTINDALE

HAYESWATER AND
HIGH STREET

66

Sandwick
59

THE EDEN VALLEY, which forms a broad green swathe between the Cumbrian mountains and the Pennine chain, contains many features to delight the inquisitive traveller. Pendragon Castle (below) lies in Mallerstang, close to the headwaters of the Eden on the borders of Westmorland and Yorkshire.

Concentrated within the space of a few miles on the west side of the Eden near Penrith are three remarkable ancient churches—Brougham chapel, Clifton and Ninekirks (page 70). They contain many associations with local families.

A string of villages along the edge of the Pennines not far from Appleby has long been referred to as the East Fellside. The area, shown in picture map form on page 71, is remote in spirit from the hustle of modern life and is the romping ground of the famous Helm Wind.

PENDRAGON CASTLE AND WILD BOAR FELL

AD
1661

HOMINEM
TE ESSE MEMENTI

Wᵐ de Wybergh married
Elianor yᵉ only Daughter
& Sole Heir of Gilbert de
Engayne of Clifton in yᵉ
County of Weſtmorˡᵈ in yᵉ
38.of K.Edwᵈ yᵉ 3ᵈ By wᶜʰ
Elianor came yᵉ Manor of
Clifton to yᵉ Wyberghs'.
1738.

Ninekirks

Brougham
Chapel

Clifton Church

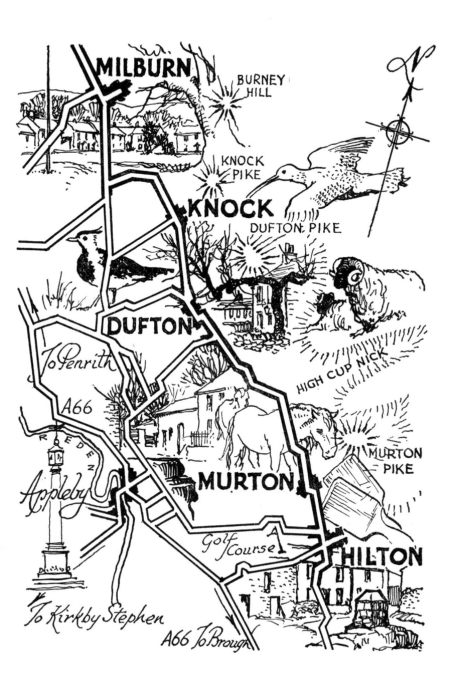

MILBURN

BURNEY HILL

KNOCK PIKE

KNOCK

DUFTON PIKE

DUFTON

To Penrith

A66

HIGH CUP NICK

EDEN

Appleby

MURTON

MURTON PIKE

Golf Course

HILTON

To Kirkby Stephen

A66 To Brough

WILD BOAR FELL from AISGILL MOOR

The last two sketches in this book were made in Mallerstang, the wonderfully-sounding name for a wonderful valley where the fells leap upon either side to an altitude of well over 2,000 feet. The summits of these are indeed quiet places, where only the bleat of the moorland sheep and the crying of the curlew disturbs the lonely silence.

e. jeffrey

ABOVE 'THE THRANG'

72